Praise for

M000190427

"Sherrie Dunlevy's journey of heartbreak and loss is a poignant one, and the story of her choice to become better rather than bitter is beautiful. She teaches us life lessons to help others in their grief, sorrow, and distress. In this book, we are all encouraged to reach out and make a difference when our family and friends are in crisis. I recommend this book to everyone!"

—Elizabeth Rose Cunningham, author of *Porch Swings & Fireflies: Creating Life After Loss*

"Life situations can be very difficult, especially the loss of a loved one. This book provides tangible things that one can do to help friends through the grieving process and beyond. I will recommend this read to my colleagues."

—Cheryl L. Jones, RN, MSN, NEA-BC, and Director, WVU Medicine Children's Hospital

"After decades of interviewing hundreds of authors, I know the two ingredients that make the best 'help' books: personal passion and simplicity. Sherrie Dunlevy brings both to *How I Can Help?* After detailing a personal tragedy that changed her approach to life, Dunlevy uses her passion to fashion a simple list of techniques readers can use to provide comfort and help to others. This passion imbues her understandable and usable techniques for helping others with its power."

—Howard Monroe, Watchdog Radio Network

"Sherrie Dunlevy's book is a simple way to fine-tune one's caregiving skills. It also answers so many questions often not asked by caregivers or their loved ones. Any caregiver or person who runs a caregiver group should add this to his or her reading list. Thank you, Sherrie, for all of your insight and care for this subject! This book comes from the heart."

—Dan Pinciaro, lifestyle and wellness coach

"Sherrie has done a skillful job in highlighting both useful *and* harmful tactics to use with grieving people. This book will help those who feel paralyzed by the fear of not knowing how to help a grieving friend."

Jamie Roberts, LPCC, grief recovery specialist, and Rev. David Roberts, grief recovery specialist

"A handbook for a time when words are spoken but often not heard and actions speak volumes that will later be remembered. Sherrie captures the true essence of grieving in situations that are out of our control; the need for support, love, and caring in all of them is greater than we realize. Loss is a real part of living. Supporting those in the grieving process, whether due to death, separation, illness, or another type of loss, not only helps the one grieving but also helps the supporter move through his or her own loss. I can see this book in so many places: Hospitals, funeral homes, and even churches will benefit from these words. Thank you for writing this!"

—Laurie Labishak, singer, songwriter, and motivational speaker

"In our age of social media, which has crowded out face-to-face conversation, many need practical advice on how to speak to others about their suffering. In this short book, Sherrie Dunlevy compiles experienced-based wisdom from those who have suffered loss to help us express our concern and offer useful help—so that the human relationships necessary for support and healing are strengthened and not severed. Dunlevy's work is honest, clear, and encouraging—an essential resource that shows us how we may always reach out courageously and lovingly to someone suffering serious loss."

—Jamey Brogan, M.Div., Director, Campus Ministry, Mission and Identity at Wheeling Jesuit University, and former Assistant Editor, *America*

"Truly, this book has encouraged me to more deeply examine my relationships with loved ones, colleagues, and even acquaintances who are faced with small struggles or the deepest despair. Sherrie's own heartfelt descriptions and insight, coupled with the accounts of people whom she thoroughly surveyed, give us concrete tools and suggestions for being the best possible companion, helper, and listener we can be. Through these stories, I am also more able to identify and appreciate those who were a blessing to me during difficult times. Life is filled with such joy and potential, but we will all face sorrow and heartache, as well. It's how we love and support one another that makes all the difference in that journey."

—Kym Gable, media personality, producer, voice artist, and talent coach

"I was very moved by Sherrie and those she interviewed as they shared their stories with me in *How Can I Help?* I believe that anyone who has ever been uncertain of how to respond when a friend or loved one has experienced a loss or serious illness will benefit from reading this book. Thank you, Sherrie, for acting on that idea that wouldn't go away."

—Cynthia Bougher, RN, CEO, Valley Hospice
(Steubenville, Ohio)

"I read this book three days after burying my fifty-three-year-old brother after his unexpected death. It offers extremely helpful, simple how-to's that can truly make a difference in the life of someone who is experiencing tragedy. I highly recommend it."

—Shari Prichard, President,
Women in the Word Ministries

"How Can I Help? provides you with a blueprint to support anyone you know who may be experiencing loss. Sherrie Dunlevy knows all too well the pitfalls of managing her own grief and the well-intentioned words she once heard as she navigated her own course to healing. In *How Can I Help*?, Sherrie shares heartfelt, actionable steps to help you support anyone in your life experiencing a loss while allowing them the dignity of their own grieving process."

—Mitch Newman, M.A., The Relationship Adviser

"One would think that the practice of pediatric cardiology would enable me to assist friends and loved ones in dealing with the tragedies of life: chronic illness, death, divorce, loss of employment and/or professional status. After all, my calling has led me to assist countless parents of terminally ill children to get through the worst of all ordeals. Unfortunately, this is not the case. Dealing compassionately with the family of a patient is different from assisting a friend in time of need. Sherrie Dunlevy's guide for helping others is remarkable for its clarity, good advice, and common sense. This book will change the way I deal with such situations in the future. Thankfully, it is never too late for a book like this to open one's eyes."

—William Neal, M.D., Professor Emeritus, Pediatrics, West Virginia University, and Past National Chair, Children's Miracle Network

"After reading *How Can I Help?*, I knew exactly what to say to someone who unexpectedly lost her best friend recently after a seventy-year relationship. Thank you, Sherrie, for showing us how to support others in the simplest, kindest way possible. Your words are timely and important."

—Jennifer Read Hawthorne, coauthor, #1 *New York Times* bestselling *Chicken Soup for the Woman's Soul* and *Chicken Soup for the Mother's Soul*

"Sherrie has answered the question *How Can I Help?* by *assisting* us in the form of her open-hearted sharing of her spirit-filled book. Thank you, my friend, for helping us help our loved ones in their time of need."

—Douglas Holzmeier, life coach, motivational speaker, radio personality, and author of *You Are God's Best Idea!*

"I am moved, convicted, and inspired all at the same time. What an incredible reminder, a true call to action to *show* love, presence, compassion, and empathy. The best of intentions are useless to a friend in need. It's a great reminder of how disconnected we truly are, in a world where we appear to be so plugged in."

—Kathi Leonard, CHC, AADP, nutrition counselor and transformation coach

HOW CAN I HELP?

Your Go-To Guide for Helping
Loved Ones through Life's Difficulties

SHERRIE DUNLEVY

SPIRIT STRIKES
PUBLISHING

Wheeling, West Virginia

Published by:

SPIRIT STRIKES
PUBLISHING

Wheeling, West Virginia

Library of Congress Cataloging-in-Publication Data available upon request.

First printing 2016

ISBN: 978-0-69282-083-4

Cover and interior: www.TheBookCouple.com

Printed in the United States of America

To the three greatest loves of my life:
Rob, Trey, and Brandon

Contents

Preface

I was eighteen weeks pregnant when my husband and I learned that our baby had a condition known as a *diaphragmatic hernia*—a condition very few children survive. Despite visits to numerous children's hospitals before he was born, there was just no guarantee he was going to make it. So we finally let people know what we were facing: He was going to be born very sick, he was going to need surgery, and he might not survive.

Brandon was born on March 29, 1999. He was immediately transported to Pittsburgh's Children's Hospital, where he was eventually put on a heart/lung machine (ECHMO). Later, he had surgery to repair the hernia. These were the most grueling days of our lives. With another young son still at home, we traveled 120 miles daily to be at Brandon's side. Since he had been born via C-section, I was not allowed to drive for a few weeks and had to rely on others to take me to see him. In addition, my husband had to return to work, and someone had to care for our two-year-old son at home.

We were blessed to have family who split their time sitting at Brandon's bedside and caring for our son Trey at home so that we could visit the hospital. They were there for us when Brandon's condition turned critical and we had to stay at the hospital by his side. In addition to transporting me to the hospital, a few friends visited us at the hospital to see our baby and to make sure we were doing OK.

We were not OK. Our baby was fighting for his life, and we had another baby at home who missed his parents and could not understand why they were not at home. We were tired, stressed, heartsick, and had never felt more helpless in all our lives.

Brandon passed away after only twenty-nine days of life. His little body could not take any more. We left the hospital for the final time and headed straight to the funeral home to make final arrangements for our child. Never would we have expected that our first dealings with a funeral home would be to plan the transport and burial of our baby. It was one of the most horrible times imaginable for us.

The funeral took place, and then it was back to life—but it had changed so very much for our family. We would not be bringing home a newborn baby. Trey would not grow up with a baby brother. The dream we had for our life had suddenly been redefined. We were parents to two children, yet only one was alive.

No one ever expects to outlive their child, and Brandon's death was something that was very difficult to understand, let alone live with. If it were not for the outpouring of love and support from our family and friends, I'm not sure we would have been able to get through this painful time as well as we did.

Suddenly, it became very important for us to keep Brandon's memory alive. We found ourselves members of a proverbial club we didn't want to be in— the "parents who've lost a child" club. But we were so grateful to find that there were other "members" who knew exactly what we were going through, as we all shared a similar experience. We joined a support group called SHARE, which is for parents who have lost a baby due to miscarriage, stillbirth, or infant death.

It was helpful to be able to talk with other parents who had gone through a similar situation; we were able to help one another deal with the many feelings and emotions surrounding the loss of our babies. This was one way in which we were able to keep our children's names and memories alive.

We also set up funds in Brandon's name at both West Virginia University Children's Hospital and Pittsburgh Children's Hospital. We were able to provide money to purchase some much needed equipment that would help those hospitals care for other infants in their neonatal intensive care units.

One such piece of equipment actually was able to

read bilirubin levels in a baby without a needle stick. This was especially meaningful to us, as Brandon had so many tubes and lines in his body that the nurses had a tough time finding new veins to stick. Watching our baby being poked and prodded every single day was excruciating for us. Even though the medical staff assured us he wasn't feeling pain, seeing needles, tubes, lines, and scars all over our son's body was very upsetting. Now, because of our donation, many babies are able to avoid this kind of pain and parents have one less needle to worry about.

It has now been many years since Brandon passed away, and we have been able to heal from the hurt and pain we experienced from his death. Time does help in the healing process. But it was the outpouring of love, care, and concern that so many people shared with us throughout our time of grieving that really helped heal our hearts. Our lives continue, and we are able to experience joy once again.

Brandon's death was something that happened in our lives; however, we have worked to make sure that our lives are not defined by his death. Our lives have forever changed, but we have been able to see the blessing that was Brandon. We are grateful for the gift of our son and the many lessons his life and his death have given us.

It is my heartfelt hope that sharing our family's story will encourage others to step up and help in times of crisis.

Acknowledgments

Have you ever had an idea that comes on strong and then won't go away—one that gnaws at and pesters you until you finally just have to do something about it? I have, and this book is the result of that idea.

I am a former news anchor, a radio talk show host, and a businesswoman. I am not an author—or, more accurately, I was not an author until now. But this book is the result of an idea that hit me and needed to be born. It is my first experience of what I have begun calling "spirit strikes." I feel as though I have become a vessel through which spiritual messages flow.

That said, I would like to acknowledge the Holy Spirit for the inspiration to create something It obviously thinks the world needs. I would also like to thank the people who have helped me get this written, edited, and published. Janet Boyle, thank you for your interest in this project and for your help in getting me started by encouraging me to believe that there was a need for this type of book. Toni Brancazio, thank you for your help in getting me from paper to computer and everything in between.

To my editor, Jennifer Read Hawthorne, thank you for making my words on the page match exactly the message that was in my head and heart.

Daniel Caron, The Nature Nomad, your incredible image, which graces my book cover, perfectly conveys the complexity of life. It proves that even with life's unexpected twists, beauty can still exist! Gary Rosenberg, you incorporated this image and my vision into a perfect cover; I am so very grateful.

I thank my extended family, who have loved my husband, son, and me unconditionally through this process and who offered us the support we needed to stay afloat during the most challenging time of our lives.

*"Our prime purpose in this life
is to help others. And if you can't
help them, at least don't hurt them.*

—DALAI LAMA

Introduction

Life is hard. You've heard it said time and time again. The truth is, however, it's not just a saying. Life IS hard, unpredictable, and many other things. Not all the time, but it has its moments—and when they hit, they can be devastating.

Death, illness, unemployment, and divorce are some of the most difficult problems people face every day. Some people lose their jobs; others face losing their homes. Some people are diagnosed with terminal illnesses. Others have just lost the love of their life. These devastating blows can send even the strongest person into a downward spiral of grief, sorrow, and depression.

Take a look around. Have you seen any of these people? Do you know any of these people? Are you one of these people?

The fact is, no one is immune to the bad things in life. Some people might face one or two of these tragedies in their lifetime; others may experience many.

The question is, Will the person be able to steer the vehicle along the road to recovery when she hits one of these major bumps, or will she crash because her life has taken an unexpected and horrifying turn?

Life is full of ups and downs, good times and bad times. Much of life is lived in between those highs and lows. It's easy and fun being friends when life is good, and the experiences you share with a friend are great. But what happens when tragedy hits? What if a friend's husband is killed in a car accident? What happens when your best friend just found out he has cancer? That's when you find out the true depth of your friendship. When it changes from fun, free, and easy to complicated, messy, and devastating, you'll learn the true strength of the friendship. Bad times can severely test a friendship. Many people who have gone through some of the most traumatic times of their lives say they were devastated when people they thought were their dear friends disappeared when they needed them the most or acted as if nothing traumatic had happened. Many friendships that were once seen as solid simply collapsed because things got tough.

Be assured of this:

- These situations are never forgotten.

- The pain never goes away.

- These situations can ruin friendships forever.

Time and time again, I have heard people who have experienced a tragedy say that they found out who their true friends were when that happened. Many were hurt when someone they felt closest to abandoned them, while others were quite surprised by and grateful for the love and support offered to them by those they considered just social friends or acquaintances.

When tragedy strikes someone you love, you will have to decide what kind of friend you will be: one who is there every step of the way or one who looks the other way. I believe the tips and suggestions offered in this book are some of the most helpful you'll find anywhere. That's because the answers come from people who have actually gone through very difficult experiences. These people have suffered the loss of children, spouses, parents, and siblings. They have been diagnosed with chronic and terminal illnesses. They have lost jobs, gotten divorced, or survived sudden changes in their lives due to accidents, crime, or natural disasters. They have walked through fire and have come out the other side permanently changed. Without exception, they say they got through those trying times thanks in part to the help of their loved ones. And that, dear readers, is my intention behind writing this book: LOVE and a call to action based on love.

Who Can Benefit from This Book

If you really feel a calling to help someone in need but are at a loss for what to do, or if you're afraid that what you do or say might somehow be wrong for someone—causing them to feel worse than they're already feeling—then this book was written for you!

There is no one preferred way of reading this book. You can read it cover to cover or you can flip through the pages, find the situation with which you need assistance, and go directly to that section to find a suggestion or two that best fits your circumstances and comfort level. You might also look for something that you know the other person who needs help would love.

During a conversation with my dear friend Kathi, in which we were talking about my writing this book, she shared with me that a friend of hers had suffered a loss. Kathi wanted to give her friend space to process her grief without interfering. That's when I told her that letting someone know you care is NOT interfering. It is showing love.

Here's the thing: There are all kinds of reasons we delay taking action. If you only take away one lesson from this book, I pray it will be this: You can *never* go wrong when you act with an open heart full of love. It will be virtually impossible to say or do the wrong things.

This book is meant to be a lesson in Loving, Caring, and Sharing. It provides that lesson in the following ways:

- It lets you know that what you do matters.

- It encourages you to step up and reach out.

- It shows you that any kind word or action will help in the healing process.

- It shows you that LOVE is what it is all about—what this life is all about.

To gather useful information about how to show others love in times of crisis, I surveyed people I knew who had experienced tragedy like the death of a loved one, the loss of a marriage or partnership, or the loss of a job. Many of these people are still healing. Many will tell you the pain never goes away, yet all of them have stories about the love and care that was shown them—stories filled with wonderful ideas and suggestions that you can use when it's time for you to step up and help.

What This Book Is About

When tragedy strikes someone near and dear to them, some people are able to kick their support into high gear. They never give it a second thought—they just see a need and do their best to fill it. It seems as if they know the perfect thing to do and begin to execute their plan right away. These folks really have no need for this book. Such people just seem to have either that natural ability to take charge of a situation or the kind of nurturing personality that automatically kicks in when needed.

But you may not have these abilities. Sometimes the emotion surrounding the situation or event is so overpowering that it can render you feeling helpless as to what to do. It can be incredibly difficult to see someone you love or care about suffer. You want to do something—anything—that will help relieve them of their pain, but you're so afraid of saying or doing the wrong thing. You may also have feelings of helplessness. You know you can't make it all better. You know you can't turn back the hands of time to prevent the painful event from ever happening at all. You definitely don't want to add to that person's pain. So the safest option, you might think, is to do nothing at all.

Or you may have the best intentions to help but you may keep putting it off. You may say to yourself, "I don't want to interfere with their life right now," or "I'll wait until their family leaves." Then, before you know it, you realize you've waited too long. What people *intend* to do and what they *actually* do can often be two different things. When someone you love is hurting, **intentions mean nothing; actions mean everything.** Lack of action can be detrimental to your friendship or relationship if you are not there when your loved one needs you most. **That** they will not forget. **Ever!** In fact, your lack of action could actually **add** to their suffering. They need *you* to turn to, and *you* need to be there.

The good news is this: You can help. There is always something you can do to show your support to those people you love. But how exactly can you help? What specifically can you do? What should you say? These are the questions many people ask in these kinds of situations, and the answers can be found in this book. This book was written as a go-to guide to providing comfort to the people you care about when they are going through a difficult time.

It might seem odd that there needs to be a book to help you help others deal with life's tragedies. But believe me, as a person who suffered the loss of a child, I can tell you that this is a much needed book. During the worst time of our lives, my husband and I had some very close friends practically disappear from our lives. Friends who were in our wedding and had celebrated our life's greatest moments simply dropped out of our lives when we needed their love and support the most. As a result, we felt hurt and abandoned, and most of all, we just couldn't understand why they would not reach out to us. It damaged, if not ruined, our relationships with them. We didn't know if it was just too awkward, too painful, or too sad for them, but we were counting on their support and did not get it. Not then, not ever. They simply disappeared from our lives. It was as if there had never been a friendship at all.

Maybe they didn't know what to say.

Maybe they didn't know what to do.

Maybe they were afraid if they got too close it could happen to them.

Maybe if they had had a book like this, they could have been there when we, their friends, needed them most.

It is now, many years later, that I realize there may be a pattern to this. You see someone going through a difficult time. You don't know what to say or do, or you're afraid you'll say or do the wrong thing, and so you do nothing. Then time passes and you feel bad that your friend or loved one didn't have your support. Instead of calling and apologizing, you continue to stay away. Years of friendship are wiped away because you let fear, embarrassment, or regret keep you from acting in love.

It is my hope that this book will put an end to that fear.

If you don't know what to say or do, continue reading this book. It has been written just for you, and the people who have contributed to it tell you specifically what helped them the most in their times of need. The book is broken down into sections that deal with some of life's most difficult situations. Each section has actions you can take that may help your loved one, words that might make you feel more comfortable talking to them, and some words and actions that you might want to avoid. In Chapter 1, we'll talk about how our world has changed and how that affects the way we support our loved ones. In Chapter 2, we'll talk about how to support people through death. In Chapter 3, we'll talk about helping people through terminal or chronic illness and disability, and in Chapter 4, we'll talk about helping people through divorce and unemployment. Finally, in Chapter 5, we'll talk about the two most important actions you can take in any of these situations to help others heal.

The suggestions made in this book come from people who found comfort when they were suffering. I hope you will read it, find one or a few recommendations that work for you, and help a friend heal.

Remember, it is never too late, and your help in a time of crisis will always be remembered and appreciated.

*"No one is useless in this world
who lightens the burdens of another."*

—Charles Dickens

CHAPTER 1

Our Changing World

This book is probably needed more at this time in history than ever before. Times and circumstances have changed dramatically. Technology has made it easier for us to communicate with each other. We can now Skype or FaceTime through our computers and phones with people all over the world for free. And yet, at the same time, many of us have our heads so deeply buried in that same technology that it is actually detrimental to face-to-face communication. We are now able to chat with someone on the other side of the world, and yet we don't even know our next door neighbor, let alone carry on a conversation with her.

Our lives are made better by the relationships we have. The connections we have to one another are critical, yet too many times those connections are missing. As a result, some people have absolutely no idea what to do, what to say, or even how to broach the subject with someone who is experiencing a tragedy in their life.

Back in the day, when someone was dealing with a difficult situation, there were many sources of support to help them through it. A few of the strongest ones that

I can recall from my childhood were extended family, neighbors, friends, and the "church ladies." But today, the advent of technology has completely altered the way many of us communicate and interact with each other. As a result, a lot of these support systems are no longer in place. It isn't so much that people don't care. It's that times and the way we live our lives have changed. Let's take a look at these traditional support systems and some of the key changes that have affected them.

Extended Family

It used to be that families lived in very close proximity to each other. When people needed help, they could rely on family members to pitch in and take care of things. Grandparents could watch the kids at home. Aunts could send over dinner. Uncles could mow the lawn.

These days, many families are spread out all over the country. Family members are so far away they have to Skype to visit their grandchildren. So when a tragedy occurs, it's not as simple as running next door or getting in your car and driving a few blocks to be able to pitch in and help. Now you have to plan trips by plane, train, and automobile—trips that can take anywhere from a few hours to a few days. Some people have to arrange leave from work, and others may not have the time or resources available to be there to provide support.

When family members are separated by hundreds or thousands of miles, it's not so easy for an aunt come over and sit with the kids, for a single mom to drop everything to rush home to her father's side when he's fallen ill, or for a father living apart from his children to take over should his ex-wife have to leave town.

Neighbors and Friends

Neighborhoods have changed too. Many can remember the days of children riding their bikes on the sidewalks, neighbors sitting out on their front porch swings or gliders, and folks just dropping by for a visit. Neighbors used to look after each other's children, and neighborhood children used to run errands for the widow down the street.

As the saying goes, "It takes a village to raise a child." But that is more challenging in today's world than it was previously. Moms who once might have stayed home with the kids are now out earning a paycheck. Children who used to hang out with other kids in the neighborhood playing dolls, kickball, or hide-and-seek don't have the time; they're never home because they are overscheduled with activities. And the widow down the street is now in a nursing home because her family lives too far away to make sure she's OK.

Today, many are lucky to even know their neighbors. The following is an example of many Americans' typical day: They go to the garage, get in the car, open the garage door, back the car out, remotely shut the door, and go to work. When they leave work, they drive directly into their garage and walk into their house. They travel from home to work and work to home without ever having come in contact with a neighbor.

Sidewalks and front porches have now been replaced by back decks, keeping people further secluded from one another. Our need for privacy is actually cutting the lifeline to our neighborhoods.

Friends, like family members, can be spread out all over the country and living lives that are equally challenging. Most women are out in the workforce while raising a family, severely limiting how much time they are able to spend with others. Family schedules, work commitments, and little downtime make it next to impossible to drop everything in a time of crisis. But while that is the reality for many, it should not be an excuse to do nothing.

Church Ladies

Church ladies were the dear women who were stay-at-home moms, homeroom mothers, and of course, caretakers of the church. They were the women you knew you could count on no matter what—the "go-to girls" who took control and set things in motion when someone in the congregation was suffering. Their help eased the burden of grieving families.

While these women still exist, their ranks are thin due to the limits of time and money. Many of today's women have jobs—some by choice, most by necessity. Between working and caring for their families, it's simply not possible for most women to take a day off work and volunteer to cook a funeral luncheon for a parish member.

While many churches continue this ministry, many do not have the necessary resources. "Church lady duties" have been reduced to monetary donations made so that catered dinners can be supplied to the grieving families. The bellies of the grieving may be full, but that special tender loving care provided by this wonderful ministry is missing. Add to that the fact that many people are no longer associated with an organized religion and may not belong to a church community, and when such people are going through a tragic event, their support system might be even smaller.

Technology: The Game Changer

The world of technology also has a lot to do with how we interact with our friends and neighbors, if we choose to do so at all. Thanks to today's technology, it is entirely possible that a person can have all her needs met without ever having to interact with anyone. Is this possible? Yes. Is this healthy? You decide.

It is now possible to shop online, never needing to set foot in a store and having everything delivered right to your doorstep, all without having to talk or interact with anyone.

Personal touches like handwritten letters and notes have been replaced by e-mails; phone calls have been replaced by texts. These methods are quick, convenient, and efficient—although many people would say much less personal.

Look at today's children. Most of their interactions are performed electronically. They socialize via social networks instead of at bowling alleys or pizza shops. In fact, it's not all that uncommon that when you spot a group of teens or young adults who are actually out socializing with each other in person, each member of the group will be burying his head in his smartphone instead of talking and laughing with the others. Instead of flapping their gums, they will be moving their thumbs with quick precision as they communicate with each other via text.

This is definitely a *different* way of communicating and interacting, but different does not always mean worse. As long as people are using technology to get to know one another better instead of to isolate themselves, then I think interacting via technology has its place in helping and healing. However, keep in mind that tone and intent can be misconstrued when offering condolences or sympathy in a short text.

High Tech ≠ High Touch

The dynamics of the family, the neighborhood, and the church have changed. Technology has changed the way many interact. But the way we suffer and the way we heal has not changed. The need for connection, love, and support has not gone away.

These changes do, however, make it much more challenging to get the help we so desperately need in difficult times. We need each other, we need support, and we need love—and therefore, we need to support and love those who are hurting.

So what can we do in these changing times to support others? Let's look first at what to do when a friend loses a loved one.

*"Never underestimate the difference
YOU can make in the lives of others.
Step forward, reach out, and help.
This week reach to someone that
might need a lift."*

—Pablo

CHAPTER 2

When a Loved One Dies

The thought of death can be overwhelming, scary, and even debilitating for many people. And because of this, some choose not to think about it at all. But this technique is not going to change the fact that everyone is going to die and that most likely, all of us will face losing someone we love.

For those who have a difficult time even thinking about death, dealing with the death of a loved one can be catastrophic. Many people block it completely out of their minds because facing the finality of death is just too scary. Questions such as *What happens when one dies? Is it painful? Where do you go?* can make you feel scared and uncomfortable.

And when someone you love dies, you come to realize you will never see them, talk to them, or hold them ever again. It's extremely painful to even think about, so imagine what it feels like when someone you love is facing such a loss. Imagine how much they might be hurting.

When someone loses a loved one, they are often not prepared for what is happening. For some, it is a sudden traumatic situation such as an unexpected death; their family member or friend was fine one minute and gone the next. It's shocking, and often, those left behind are not only trying to process what has just happened, but also dealing with thoughts of what they might have left unsaid or unresolved with the person who has suddenly died. For others, it's watching someone they love suffer, either from a debilitating condition or a long, lingering disease. So when death comes, it can seem to be a relief that the deceased person's suffering is over. Those left behind might have had time to say everything they needed to say to the person who died, but still, they're grieving.

Death is not a topic people should dwell on, yet it's not something they should ignore. So when it happens, having someone to help them through their grieving is one of life's greatest gifts. It's a gift you can give them out of love and one that they will appreciate forever. You can give them that gift by showing up to help them bear the sorrow, letting them lean on you in weak moments, and talking with them about their loss.

When people suffer a loss, they are dealing with feelings of grief, denial, anger, sadness, and confusion. Some are experiencing emotions they have never before encountered, and most of them are terrified. That is why it is so important to offer them all the love, care, and support you can.

I have had the opportunity to talk with people who have lost loved ones to illnesses, suicide, and accidents. They have so many stories to share of things their friends and loved ones did to help them navigate the waters of shock and sorrow. So what can you do or say that will help a loved one deal with death? Here are some specific tips and suggestions from people who shared their stories with me.

Be There

Every single person surveyed for this book listed "being there" as what was most important to them. If you are close to the person who is suffering from a loss or other tragedy, just being with them so they are not alone is not only important but crucial in helping them through this unsettled time of their life.

Your presence is all that is required. No words, no actions—just BE.

Be present for them, listen to them, hold their hand, let them cry, or cry with them. When you are with them, they know they do not have to face their loss alone. Some may want to talk and others may not, but all agree that knowing someone is there is very important.

Jody, who lost her sister to breast cancer, says she was blessed with the love and support she received from her friends. "My lifelong best friend from Atlanta showed up the day after my sister passed and stayed with me throughout her funeral. She took care of getting the food together since everyone congregated at my house, kept the house straightened up, and was there in the middle of the night when I would fall apart." She adds, "I really had exceptional friends that left nothing unsaid or undone for us."

Judy says the sudden death of her husband was the most traumatic experience of her life. She is grateful for a dear friend who immediately traveled hundreds of miles to be at her side. She says, "She took over my entire life and allowed me to rest and try to sleep and use her as a sounding board through all my ranting and monologues that I spouted endlessly."

Jody offers this advice for helping others dealing with the death of a loved one: "Let them know you're there; get them out among the living—be relentless if necessary. And do not disappear after the funeral—that is when the real loss sets in and *precisely* when people need their loved ones the most."

Brady, who lost her sister Erin to cancer, agrees that keeping in touch after the funeral is so important. "Once the funeral is over, everyone stops coming around and calling. I know everyone must move along and get on with life, but the people who did still call and keep in touch really meant a lot."

Be prepared that your friend may not be himself or herself. Trying to process losing someone he or she loves can be mind-boggling. Some people feel as though their world has been turned upside down, and their focus therefore won't always be on what is going on around them. Some people lose all track of time in the first few days. They become confused about the time of day, the day of the week, or even the month of the year. They may not know if it's Monday or Tuesday or if it's morning or night: all they know is that someone is there with them. But when they look back at that confusing time, the one thing they will be able to recall is whether they were feeling abandoned and alone or whether they were feeling grateful for being supported in a loving manner.

Listen

When people suffer a loss, they tend to run it through their minds almost endlessly; part of the grieving process is talking about it over and over and over. Some might want to tell you how it happened or how their loved one was discovered, while others might recall a favorite memory.

Please remember to be patient with them. Keep in mind that your grieving friends or relatives are going through a very traumatic time. They're trying to make sense of the fact that just yesterday, their loved one was alive, but today, he or she is dead. It could have been a sudden death, which still seems impossible to believe, or it could have been a long, drawn-out process about which every detail from diagnosis to death is crystal clear. Just let your grieving friends talk, process, and remember, because having someone there to listen without interruption is very important and always remembered later. Almost every person who responded to the survey listed a friend or loved one who would simply listen as one of the things they needed most.

Lori, who lost a childhood friend to suicide, said, "Just listening helps a lot. Listen and let them get it out." Whether it's in person, by phone, or by Skype, let them do the talking and just lend an ear.

Don't be surprised to find people experiencing many emotions all at once. Those who are grieving can express anger, sadness, and guilt even as they are laughing. It is not your job to try to help them calm down—just be there while they "feel" their way through these conflicting emotions so they can get them out of their system.

You needn't worry that you don't know what to say; sometimes, no words are necessary. In fact, Jody put it this way: "There are not many people who are going to offer profound enough words to ease the pain. Don't feel you need to do this. A simple and sincere "I'm so sorry!" is often enough."

Again, for those who grieve, repeating things may be necessary; just let them talk, process, and remember.

Send Food and Drinks

When there is a death, many decisions have to be made. They range from buying a cemetery plot to writing an obituary, from picking out clothes for the deceased to dealing with the funeral arrangements. Remembering to eat, let alone deciding what to eat, rarely comes to mind. Sending a meal to the house of your loved one really helps because it gives them one less detail to attend to. It can be a favorite recipe for some immediate comfort food or a casserole that can be frozen and used at a later date. If you don't cook, buy a bucket of chicken and some macaroni salad, send a luncheon tray with buns and condiments, or deliver a vegetable or fruit tray. Having prepared food on hand allows easy access to a meal at any time of day.

Another suggestion that not many think of is breakfast food. Sending a breakfast casserole or a tray of Danish makes it convenient for the family to eat something first thing in the morning. Your thoughtfulness can help get them through what likely will be a very long day. When Marianne lost her mother, one of the things she appreciated the most was the breakfast basket that a friend sent to her. "It had everything in the basket—napkins, individual cereals, milk, muffins, flavored coffee, and flavored cream cheese, along with a bouquet of flowers for my table."

If a lot of food is being sent to the house, you may want to consider drinks and ice. With guests streaming in and out of the house during this time, there is always the need for a cold drink or a cup of coffee.

It also helps to include cups, napkins, plates, and eating utensils. Not only will these be needed, but they'll be most appreciated when it's time to clean up. Simply throwing everything away is much easier than having dishes and glasses stacking up.

Many families have one-day funeral viewings with perhaps a short one- or two-hour break between sessions. You may want to call the funeral home and see if you can send over food and/or drinks for the family to help them through their day.

Pray

If you are a person of faith, sending up a prayer for your loved one is something you can do anytime, anywhere. Most people surveyed said that just knowing others were praying for them gave them strength.

Anne, who lost her father, said this about prayer: "That someone would care enough to pray is overwhelming, and sometimes when you're experiencing traumatic times, you have no ability to pray yourself. So that's the time you desperately need the prayers of others."

Nancy, who tragically lost her father, mother, and brother all within a few years of each other, says that knowing others are praying for you is very important. "It makes me know people want to help, even if there is nothing they can do physically. God will do what needs to be done, but it is nice to know you have others in your corner."

Many others say knowing people are praying provides comfort and restores hope.

Send Condolences

Sending sympathy cards is one way to show someone you're thinking of them. A card is something tangible one can read over again and perhaps keep in a special place. Make sure to include a small note when you send a card; it makes it so much more personal than just signing your name. Simply letting the person know you are thinking of them or jotting down a special memory of the deceased adds extra meaning to this simple act of caring.

As technology has advanced, electronic condolences have gained popularity. Many funeral homes now have websites through which messages can be sent to the family of the deceased. Other people reach out via social networks to convey sympathy. Is one method more "proper" than the other? It depends on whom you ask. The majority of survey respondents said they preferred receiving traditional cards and notes. They said getting a card or note in the mail was much more meaningful because of the extra effort the person took to shop for, write, stamp, and mail it. In addition, many said they still have many of these notes and cards as sentimental keepsakes. A few of the respondents said they felt receiving an e-mail was just a bit too impersonal.

A growing number of people find a sympathetic e-mail acceptable and believe it's definitely better than not receiving anything. However, this opinion in favor of electronic condolences was expressed mostly by younger people who have grown up communicating in this manner. Regardless of your opinion on its appropriateness, there can also be a drawback to this method—the receiver may not get your condolence message at all if it lands in a junk mail file.

Call

Making a phone call is a great way to show you care, but many avoid this action because they're afraid they won't know what to say or that they might say the wrong thing. You should not let that stop you because those phone calls are appreciated. Chances are the person won't be up for a conversation, but your reaching out will mean a lot to them regardless.

Many times, the person will not even answer the phone. If that's the case, just leave a quick message letting them know you are thinking of them. You can offer some kind of help or assistance, or you can just let them know you will check back with them a little later. And then do just that. Follow up with another phone call in a few days.

Many times, people who reach out via the phone may perceive a lack of response as a rejection. That is most likely not the case. Not everyone grieves the same way. While some might want to talk about their loved one or what they're experiencing, others might just not have the strength to tell their story one more time. Remember this is not about you; it's about helping someone you love and care about to navigate through a very difficult time. Don't worry about bothering them. As long as you keep your calls brief and you're not calling all the time, your efforts will be appreciated.

Other Helpful Suggestions

Here is a list of other things you may want to consider doing to help someone who is dealing with a death in their family:

- **Shop for groceries.** You can make a list of basic items like bread, milk, cereal, laundry detergent, toilet paper, etc., and go to the store and purchase them—or you can ask what your friend needs and fill out a list together. Sometimes, in the throes of grief, people are not thinking clearly, so don't be surprised if they're not even sure what they need. You might want to check with other family members or do some checking yourself. Then have the items delivered or deliver them yourself to their home.

- **Run errands.** Do relatives need to be picked up at the airport? Do clothes need a trip to the dry cleaner? Are there beds to be made? Can you offer an extra bedroom for out-of-town relatives? These are the kinds of extra things that may be overlooked during this time. How nice it would be if there were someone who not only thought about those details but who would take care of them too!

- **Babysit.** Sometimes, it's difficult to talk with guests while tending to small children during visitation hours. Offering to watch over the children at the funeral home could be a big help. You could either entertain the children with crayons, paper, and coloring books in a back room of the funeral parlor or see if the funeral home has the equipment to let children watch a movie. You could also offer to keep the children in your home while folks are at the funeral home.

- **Care for pets.** Does your friend or loved one have a pet? Is it being fed, walked, and taken outside to relieve itself? You could offer to take care of this.

- **Make phone calls.** Sometimes, friends and relatives from out of town need to be notified at the time of death and again once the arrangements have been made. You could offer to make some of those calls.

- **Do housecleaning.** Relatives may be coming in from out of town. You can offer to clean the bathrooms or make up the beds in the guest room to help prepare the house for visitors. These are all things that need to be done and are often not thought about until it's time to go to bed. And there will be more cleaning up to do once the funeral is over and the guests have left town. A house full of eating, drinking, and visiting people can add up to a lot of mess to deal with once everyone has gone. You may also consider hiring a company to come in and clean the home after everything is over.

- **Do laundry.** You can check to see if laundry is piled up and offer to do a load or two. If people are in from out of town, there will be towels, bedclothes, and other things that need to be laundered.

- **House-sit.** Many people like to deliver food for the family to eat after the funeral. Having someone at the house allows people to drop off food and other items for the family at any time. In addition to that, having someone at the house can prevent robberies. It's a shame that those who are grieving even have to think about it, but it's a fact that criminals comb through the obituaries to find a house with no one at home. Many families have been known to return from the cemetery only to find they have been robbed.

- **Create a gift.** Use your gifts or talents to create a lasting memory. Because my son Brandon was just a month old when he passed away, he had very few belongings and so each of them had incredible meaning for his father and me. A family friend went to his woodshop and created the most beautiful memory box for us. It is a treasure that holds the few objects that remind us of our son. Another friend who was an artist sent a print of a beautiful tree in full bloom that adds beauty to our home. I look at it daily and am reminded of his personal act of kindness and compassion. I use my gift of jewelry making to create keepsake bracelets with healing natural stones and angel wing charms for friends and family members mourning a loved one. Use the gifts and talents you have to create a keepsake or something that can bring a smile to the face of someone going through so much pain.

After the Funeral

Being with a friend throughout the funeral process is very important, but many say it is after the funeral when friendship can mean the most. When a family member dies, there is the shock and sorrow of the death, coupled with all the funeral arrangements that have to be made in a very short time. Family members can help with a lot of the planning, and friends can be around to provide food and help at this time. But once the funeral is over, the food has been eaten, the kitchen has been cleaned up, and family and friends have returned to their homes, reality sets in. Many people say the death really never hits them until everything is over. Some may need time to grieve in peace, which is very normal. However, loneliness can set in rather quickly, and they might need a friend more then than at any other time.

So what can you do to help your friend or loved one once everything is over and they find themselves alone? Here are some suggestions:

- **Make a phone call.** Making a short phone call to simply check in on your friend can be very helpful. This lets them know you are thinking of them and allows you to find out if they need anything and to gauge how they're doing. If you have the time and they're in a talking mood, allow them to tell their story. You can also leave a message on their machine. On the other hand, if you find yourself calling frequently and notice they're not answering at all, you may want to check on them with a visit or talk to a family member about your concerns.

- **Invite them to dinner.** Having dinner and conversation with a grieving friend is a great way to help them. It's a night they don't have to cook, and it gets them out of the house and engaged with other people for a while. In addition, someone who is grieving often does not feel like eating, let alone cooking, and they may dread cooking now because they are cooking for one less person or because the person who used to do the cooking is no longer there. Whether you want to offer a good home-cooked meal at your home or a night out at their favorite restaurant, your thoughtfulness will be greatly appreciated. If you live close by, you might even offer to send over dinner a few nights a week or organize a group of friends to pitch in.

- **Keep in touch.** Don't let your initial outreach be the last contact you make with your grieving friend or loved one. Let them know you are still thinking of them and want them to heal. You can make a quick call, send a short note, or make plans to visit. Be patient and persistent. It may take weeks or months for someone to feel like getting back into the swing of life, but it will eventually happen.

- **Remember the dates.** The first year after a death is very difficult for many people to navigate. It is the first time Christmas will be celebrated without a loved one—or it may be the first time ever that, because of their loss, they don't celebrate Christmas at all. The first Mother's Day or Father's Day without Mom or Dad can be very depressing, but these days will be quite excruciating for a mom or dad who recently lost a child. The departed loved one's birthday will pass without a celebration, and then comes the one-year anniversary of the death.

For someone suffering from a loss, these are days that are full of mixed emotions. They become dreaded dates on the calendar, and when they do arrive, many people are flooded with memories and strong feelings.

During that first year, I was never so touched as when relatives sent us cards on Brandon's birthday. They remembered! My sister still to this day sends a card every year to let us know she has never forgotten him. This one small gesture on her part means the world to my husband and me. We also have friends who have sent flowers or plants on the anniversary of Brandon's death to let us know they are thinking of us. These kind acts of theirs will stay with us forever.

Not-So-Helpful Actions

While most people I talked with said they had been overwhelmingly blessed with the comfort and support they received from family and friends after a death, they also said that family and friends said, did, or omitted a few things in ways that were more hurtful than helpful. Some were gracious enough to share these painful experiences with me in an effort to help others avoid similar discomfort.

Here are some of the actions that were more hurtful than helpful. We'll talk about unhelpful words in the next section.

Not Showing Up for the Visitation and/or the Funeral

When Marianne lost her mother, she looked for certain people to be there for her. Some were; some weren't.

Don't base your decision to attend a funeral or wake on how well you knew the deceased. Base it on the relationship you have with their loved ones. Many people believe that the funeral is more for the surviving loved ones because they need closure and the support of their family, friends, and the members of their community.

If there is a legitimate reason you can't make it to the funeral home or the wake, make sure to let your friend or relative know why you won't be there. Simply not showing up can lead people to come to their own conclusions as to why you weren't there—one of the main reasons they'll come up with in their own minds is that they didn't matter enough to you. That can be very painful at a time when they find themselves vulnerable. Marianne said it really meant a lot to see how many people cared about her when they took the time to stop to pay their respects to her mother.

Some situations make people feel so uncomfortable that they just can't face going to the funeral home or funeral. Seeing the dead body of someone you once knew can be frightening, or it might trigger a memory involving a loved one who passed. Granted, going to a funeral home is not the most pleasant experience, but you should not let that stop you from showing up. If you do not want to visit the body, don't. You can still pay your respects and pass along fond memories to loved ones without ever having to approach the casket. In fact, oftentimes, there isn't a body to be viewed at the funeral home. Videos and pictures might be displayed that will trigger great memories of the deceased or help you to remember a story to share with their family members.

Those left behind need your support. Be willing to endure a few hours of your own discomfort in order to provide comfort to the grieving. If you don't, you could so hurt someone you love that you will lose a valued relationship with them. People don't forget who was "not there" for them when they needed them the most.

Ignoring Loss Based on Your Own Value Judgments

Families come in all shapes and sizes these days. Couples today are made up of partners, companions, and spouses. Families may include people of all races, sexes, and creeds. There is no one way to describe a family other than as a group of people who live together and love one another. And when someone in your family dies, be it a traditional or nontraditional family, it hurts just the same.

Misty explains that it was very hurtful when people did not even acknowledge the loss of the man she considered her stepfather in what she describes as her nontraditional family. "Because my mom was not married to this man and he was not my official stepfather, some people did not acknowledge our grief. This was devastating. This man was as much a part of our family as my blood relatives," she said. "Love is love, regardless of blood relations or marital status."

Making Comments about Funeral Arrangements (or the Lack Thereof)

These days, people make different choices when it comes to funeral arrangements. So you might want to think twice before you start whispering about whether it was proper that the casket was open or closed, that the service was held in a church or a funeral parlor, or that there was no service at all. Many people arrange their funeral years in advance, and what you see could be exactly what that the deceased wanted or what makes the process of grieving easiest for the family. Remember, too, that many of these decisions come at a time when it is difficult to think things through, so some details may fall through the cracks. There may even be differences in opinions or family drama surrounding funerals.

It is not your place to get involved or even comment on what you think is proper. Besides, is this really the right time to be critical? When grieving friends and relatives are at their most vulnerable, offer your support and hold back on the criticism.

Being Too Quick to Change the Subject

Many people feel that if they change the subject when their friend or relative starts talking about death, it will help lessen their pain. How many times have you heard or even said, "Oh, please don't cry because if you start crying, then I'll start crying!"?

Healing comes from talking, venting, remembering, and crying. This is all a part of healthy healing. A strong, willing shoulder to cry on is often needed most. No answer is necessary, nor is one expected. So let them talk, vent, and cry; it will be the fastest way for them to feel better. Remember, people can only get *through* their grief—they can't go above, under, or around it. So allow it to happen by providing a willing ear.

Giving Your Opinion of the Cause of Death

People always seem to be extremely curious about what caused someone to die. Sometimes the reason is obvious: cancer, heart attack, car accident, etc. But sometimes the family may not want to share that information. If that's the case, leave it be. It is really none of your business, and playing detective to try and figure it out is not only rude, but very hurtful. Perhaps the deceased perished in a way that would have been embarrassing; perhaps they had a disease they didn't want anyone to know about—or perhaps they had a mental illness, which, unfortunately, is still stigmatized in this country.

One of the most devastating deaths to understand is suicide. The thought that someone is so troubled that they see the end of their life as the only solution seems unimaginable to so many of us. Yet people take their own lives daily and leave behind loved ones who may be riddled with guilt and shame and who may have questions that may never be answered.

Charmaine suffered tremendously following her father's suicide. Not only did she have to deal with the loss of her father, but she had to deal with other people's judgment. Most hurtful was when people told her that her father was now in hell. She said she is grateful that her priest was comforting and not judgmental at this extremely difficult time.

Being Impatient with the Person's Grieving Process

Although there are stages of grief, there is no timeline for being back to one's "normal" self. In fact, many experience a "new normal" after the death of a loved one. Some people may be able to heal rather quickly; others can take years to heal. So don't expect someone to be "over it" just because you think enough time has passed.

Sometimes, someone suffering from a loss will seem to be doing really well and will then have a setback. It can happen, and they should not feel weak or inadequate because of it. Each person has their own way to grieve.

Also, don't compare them to other people you know and how they dealt with loss. Every situation and every person is different; your job is to help them heal at their own pace.

Critiquing Their Grieving Process

People grieve in so many different ways. Some cry inconsolably; some shut down emotionally; some might even feel a certain sense of relief, especially if they have seen their loved one suffer through a long illness.

Mary lost her husband following a long bout of suffering. She shared the following: "A relative said I showed no emotion. My husband had been sick so long that I had been through all the emotions, anger, and breakdowns. I now knew he was at peace and pain free. He would not have wanted me to be like that. The last week of his illness was my hardest, but a sense of comfort knowing he was not in pain was good for me."

Not-So-Helpful Words

The following phrases have also been found to be more hurtful than helpful:

"If you need anything, just let me know."

For the most part, these words are uttered with the best intentions. You would do *anything* if you just knew what to do. But the problem is, most grieving people simply don't know what they need at this time, and they are not likely to pick up the phone and ask for help. Instead of asking them what they need, perhaps it would be better to offer them suggestions as to how you might help, such as running errands, doing laundry, or driving them somewhere.

"Your loved one is better off now."

People who are mourning the loss of someone they love usually believe "better off" would be with them, not dead. One of the survey respondents, Michelle, lost her father in a plane accident. Many people told her dying that way was better because it was quick. Others said he died doing what he loved. She says the pain of loss is the same whether the death is sudden and traumatic or whether it follows a long illness. Even though he did die doing something he loved, Michelle hates the thought that her father was going down in a plane and perhaps fully aware that the end was just seconds away.

"I know what you're going through."

You don't. All situations are different. After Judy's husband died unexpectedly, she had a hard time with people saying, "I know how you feel." She said, "No, they don't know how I feel. Death—like birth, marriage, and raising children—is individual. Many of us experience the same things, but we all do it in our individual ways and our feelings are our own." You may have experienced something similar, but you don't know how someone else feels.

"You don't look upset," or "Why are you showing no emotion?"

Remember, as we said in the previous section on hurtful actions, everyone is different and the way they grieve is just as different. Don't project your mental picture of what you think is the correct or best way to grieve onto someone else.

For instance, if someone has cared for a loved one during a long illness, their grieving process and emotions have been flowing for quite some time. They may actually feel a sense of relief along with their sadness—and there is nothing wrong with them feeling that way. Until you have walked a mile in their shoes, do not judge how they are dealing with their loss.

NOTES

_____

_____

_____

_____

_____

_____

_____

_____

_____

_____

_____

_____

_____

*"The greatest healing therapy
is friendship and love."*

—Hubert H. Humphrey, Jr.

CHAPTER 3

Supporting Those with Terminal or Chronic Illness/Disability

When a loved one or a family member is terminally or chronically ill, there are many things you can do to really help them out. It's very important you show that you care for them, especially because this is often a time when many so-called friends disappear. There are several things you can do, including talking about your loved one's illness, getting community involved, understanding the "rules" of visiting, learning how to care for the caregiver, and knowing what things to avoid when a loved one is terminally or chronically ill. This chapter talks about each of these ways to support your loved one.

Don't Be Afraid to Talk!

First and foremost, maintain communication with a friend who's ill. Sometimes, a terminal illness like cancer scares people away. It's as if it's contagious. Some flee because it is simply too painful to face the sick person or the possibility that someone near and dear is dying. Some simply don't want to talk about it, or the situation makes them feel uncomfortable. Some may think to themselves, *I'll call tomorrow*—but they never do. Whatever the reason, the phone calls and visits just stop. If any of these excuses cross your mind, remember: You can't catch cancer, mental illness, or most other ailments. You'll handle the situation much better if you focus on *their* pain and what *they* are facing, rather than your feelings about it.

It's OK not to know what to say. Be honest. Tell them, "I don't know what to say, but I'm here for you." Often, people don't even want to talk about their situation—they just crave normal conversation. But if they do want to talk, be there to listen. Listen without interruption and without judgment. You may find that you don't have to say anything at all.

No one wants to be alone. Remember the AIDS epidemic? Many men suffered and died alone simply because they were stigmatized for having the "gay disease." Many had family and friends simply desert them, and others were too ashamed to ask for help.

Diane, who suffers from chronic bipolar disorder, says, "A hug is always nice when you don't know what to say. The majority of people don't like feeling alone." Talking about her illness is especially important to Diane. "I would rather they ask me about it than assume they know me," she says. "I know some people think bipolar people go out and kill people or that we're all crazy. But just like any other disease, if we find the right medication combination, we can function normally."

Doug, a cancer survivor, adds that he actually wished he had been asked "How do you feel?" more often while undergoing treatment. He said that would have allowed him to really talk about what he was facing. He did use Facebook to keep people updated on his treatments and procedures, and he said that social media allowed people he hadn't heard from in years to contact him.

A person with a terrible illness or disability is still the same person inside; it's just the conditions of their life that have changed. They may not be able to do the things they used to do, but they are still able to enjoy the love and connection of a dear friend. So don't let the fact that your friend can't bowl every Friday night anymore stop you from interacting with them. How about playing a game of cards at home or renting a movie to watch together instead?

Granted, hearing of a painful, possibly terminal diagnosis may evoke fear and sadness in you and may make you reluctant to see a person whom you admire, respect, and love looking so sick, frail, and vulnerable. But it's vital that you summon the strength to fight those feelings. So if you can, resume the same conversations you had before the diagnosis. In fact, many people say they just want to be treated normally again.

That's exactly what friends did for Beth. A breast cancer survivor who is very active in her community, Beth says that one of the best things anyone did was tell her, "I still need you to chair this committee." She says she needed that project to keep her focused on the future. Distraction is also a great healer according to Barb. Knowing that she was artistic, a friend sent her a simple coloring book and crayons after she had her leg amputated. This thoughtful present was a great mood booster for her. "Each day for an hour I would color a page. After I was done with the coloring book, I sent it back to my friend and told him it was the best thing he could have done for me."

If you happen to run into someone you haven't seen in a while and they look visibly changed by a disability or illness, don't hesitate to ask them about what happened or how they are feeling. Most of the people I interviewed said they are OK talking about their situation, as long as you come from a place of genuine care and concern versus appearing to be prying into their personal life out of morbid curiosity.

Trisha suffers from many chronic disorders and doesn't mind at all that people inquire about her illnesses. In fact, she encourages people to ask questions. She says, "I would much rather they have accurate information that originated from me than wrong information that is repeated and perpetuated through rumor or guesswork."

Having walked with crutches for most of his life

due to cerebral palsy, Dale says he would much rather people ask him about his disability than stare at him. He says, "It makes me feel like a circus freak. I want them to know I am really no different. I laugh, cry, eat, poop, and have a twisted sense of humor too. I may be trapped in a body that doesn't look like yours, but I have always tried to be an inspiration to other people and to let them know, 'It's OK. You can ask. I won't bite unless you want me to.'"

James also has cerebral palsy. He doesn't mind talking to people about it, as long as it is in an intimate, respectful way. For him, asking about his illness one-on-one is fine, but it's not OK when there are a lot of other people around. That kind of attention to his disability makes him uncomfortable.

Strength in Numbers

When a loved one or friend is sick or in need, don't feel you have to provide help all by yourself. Communities, too, can come together to help the sick and their caregivers.

When Debbie's daughter, Erin, was in the hospital with cervical cancer, the outpouring of love and support she and her family received was so appreciated. "Our community held a spaghetti dinner fundraiser for Erin." In addition to the fundraiser, Debbie said her entire church family prayed for them, made a prayer blanket for Erin, and even supplied a gas card to help pay the expenses the family incurred traveling to and from the hospital.

Many times, friends and neighbors will set up schedules for sending over meals for a family that is dealing with an illness. They might also pitch in to care for children or perform chores when the chaos of dealing with this kind of situation strikes.

Those surveyed said they felt comfort, support, and love when their community of friends reached out. Having others take the time to care about them, their needs, and the needs of their family at a time when it mattered most had a definite impact on everyone involved.

Understanding the "Rules" of Visiting

When it comes to visiting someone who is ill, whether at home or at a hospital or care center, it's probably best to check with a family member to find out if visiting is allowed and if the person is up to having visitors. For some people, having someone to talk to and laugh with is the perfect medicine and a great way to pass the time and forget about their illness for a while. Others, however, may not want anyone to see them in such a fragile state. Ask rather than assume that you know what your friend prefers. If the person is up for a visit, then make the time to go. You likely won't be spending a lot of time there, but showing up can mean a lot.

Visiting someone who is ill or dying can be very daunting. Illness takes its toll on the body, and some will look very different as the disease progresses. They may have lost weight, lost their hair, or even lost some of their memory; it may be very unsettling to see them. Add to that all the round-the-clock care, machines, tubes, and other distractions that may be present, and it can be most unpleasant.

These are the kinds of things that keep many people away. It can all be boiled down to one word: *fear*. However, this is a time when you have to remind yourself that the cost of NOT going could be much higher than that of gathering your courage and showing up. There are really not many people who love to visit the sick in the hospital, and there are those who are uncomfortable or feel awkward about it. But remember, this is not about you; it is about your friend or loved one, so visit despite these feelings.

I'll never forget that when my son was in the neonatal intensive care unit, a friend of mine who was terrified of hospitals drove over an hour to visit my husband and me and to see our son. Knowing how difficult this was for her, the fact that she "sucked it up" and came anyway meant more to me than anything else she could have done. Her willingness to push past her own fears when we needed her support did the most to show me how much she loved and cared about us.

Caring for the Caregivers

Terminal illness takes its toll on caregivers too. When dealing with the illness of a loved one, the stress can be overwhelming. Many caregivers are forced to give up their jobs to care full time for someone at home, while others may be trying to hold down a job and still be there to help with the care after work.

A lot of caregivers are deprived. They're deprived of sleep, nourishment, self-care, and friends—basically deprived of life as they once knew it. Their whole world now centers on the one who is sick. They're afraid of losing someone they love. They also face the frustration of being unable to lessen their loved one's pain or stop the progression of the disease, illness, or disability.

Oftentimes, caregivers need a break from their duties but hesitate to ask anyone to step in. Many may also need to vent their fear, frustration, and sadness, as well as their guilt for even having those feelings. Some believe they are not entitled to feel that way because, after all, they are not the one suffering from an illness or disability. But they too are suffering.

Here are some things you can do that might make life just a little easier for those who are sick or caring for the sick:

- **Send a meal.** A home-cooked meal is always a welcome treat. Someone who is ill or caring for someone who is ill might not have a lot of time to plan meals or cook. If you find yourself limited on time, you can still provide food by ordering takeout and delivering it or having it delivered. You could also send gift cards for pizza or takeout, allowing them to choose what they want to eat and when they want it.

- **Send gas cards.** Trips to and from the doctor's office or hospital and to out-of-town medical facilities can add up. You can help ease the financial burden a bit by filling up the gas tank.

- **Send grocery cards.** Costs involved in caring for yourself or someone else with a terminal or chronic illness can become overwhelming. Sometimes, doctors prescribe special diets that include foods that are natural, organic, and fresh, which are often more expensive. Providing a grocery card for a store that offers these kinds of foods is especially thoughtful. Grocery cards can be used personally by the sick or by those caring for a loved one at home or at an extended-stay facility.

- **Run errands.** Being sick or caring for the sick can be exhausting, but life goes on. Banking, grocery shopping, and picking up prescriptions—these things still need to be done. You can really help someone by offering to do something they are probably just too busy or too tired to do.

- **Babysit.** An offer to babysit while your friend goes for treatment can be a godsend, but an offer to watch the kids just so your friend can have an hour or two of peace and quiet can be just as valuable. If the children are older, you may want to invite them out for an activity like spending an afternoon at the park or going to a movie. The children will have fun and escape the tension at home, and the patient or caregiver will have some much needed rest.

- **Offer to transport kids to events or school.** Someone who is sick may be too tired to keep up with the many activities that keep their children busy. Those with weakened immune systems often can't go out in public. Offering to be a "taxi driver" can be a big help.

- **Offer caregivers a break.** Caring for an ill loved one can be a round-the-clock job with very few breaks for sleep, let alone anything else in life. An offer to take over the caregiving duties for a few hours will give that caregiver an opportunity to either rest or take some much needed time for himself.

- **Offer to clean the house or mow the lawn.** Scrubbing floors and bathrooms takes time, effort, and energy—all of which are in short supply for anyone who is sick. An offer to do light cleaning might be appreciated. Maintaining the lawn may also be a chore that simply is too strenuous for someone dealing with illness. Offering to mow the grass or to pay to have a service do it may be a great blessing.

- **Call.** Make a phone call and ask if the person is up to talking. If they are, take the time to listen to what they want to tell you. They may want to talk about what they are going through, or they may want to talk about anything other than their illness. Just let them know you called because you care, not because you wanted the latest on their diagnosis. Even if they say they don't feel like talking, knowing you are thinking of them is a real spirit booster.

- **Send cards.** Just about everyone loves a note of encouragement or a card that lets them know they are in your thoughts. Sending a card is a great way to show you care.

- **Drive.** Sometimes, medications make it impossible for someone to drive; others may simply be too sick. An offer to drive your friend to church, the doctor's office, or the mall is very helpful.

- **Take care of pets.** Pet care is a real concern for anyone who is currently disabled or facing time in a hospital or other care facility. If it is possible for you to check in on the pets daily or even house them until your friend is back on his feet again, it can really give your friend peace of mind.

- **Keep in touch via the Internet.** Many folks dealing with illnesses have weakened immune systems and can't go out in public or even have visitors. The Internet and social networking sites are great ways to keep in touch, challenge each other to games, and even have live visual conversations via a service such as Skype.

- **Pray.** You can offer prayers at your own discretion, place the person on a prayer list at your church, or offer to pray with the person. Many people take great comfort in knowing someone cares for them so much that they will pray for them or with them.

- **Watch a funny movie.** Experts agree that laughter helps people heal faster and feel better. Offer to take someone to a movie or just bring one of their favorite comedies over and watch it with them. Laughter really is great medicine.

- **Send a salon or spa certificate.** A soothing massage can melt away tension and stress in someone who is sick or caring for a sick loved one. This gift of human touch can also be very healing. A pedicure is another nice way to allow someone to relax and be cared for. Many salons and spas offer gift certificates for these kinds of services.

- **Gather friends to plan an event.** Gather friends or coworkers to plan a fundraiser to assist with medical bills or travel costs. Community events like this raise money, awareness, and the spirits not only of those who are participating, but also of the person or people who are the beneficiaries of such acts of care and kindness. When everyone works together, great things can happen and no one person bears all the responsibility.

What to Avoid

A few things are important to avoid when dealing with a loved one's illness. Although I'm sure you can think of others, three of the main ones I've received feedback on are the following:

Comparing Conditions to Your Own or Those of Someone You Know

The last thing anyone who is sick or caring for the sick needs to hear is how you or your aunt, cousin, or friend had this same condition, had major complications, and died from it. You likely have the best intentions, but try to keep your conversations as positive and hopeful as possible. Don't tell them how they will feel or what they will experience. Everyone is different, and different people may respond to treatment differently. While someone might have had a horrible experience with a certain kind of treatment or therapy, that doesn't mean everyone will. Some people never have any harsh side effects at all, so don't offer your stories of gloom and doom as they will do so much more harm than good.

Beth recalls how unsettling one such conversation was after she was diagnosed with breast cancer. "Someone whose friend had a double mastectomy told me what I was going to experience, as in 'You're going to be depressed. You're going to mourn for your lost body for years. You're going to feel powerless.' It was wrong on several levels. She herself had not been through it. She was merely playing armchair therapist."

Needless to say, this is a time when people are scared and need words of encouragement, not horror stories of what someone else experienced. So take the advice my mother always used to give me as a child: "If you can't say something nice, don't say anything at all." A good rule of thumb in these types of situations might be "If you don't have something positive to share, then zip your lips." But if you do have a story of success, healing, and growth, please share! These stories can be very encouraging as they offer HOPE!

Not Believing Their Condition Is Real

Some people think that glossing over a diagnosis might be a way to actually help the person affected. They often think, *If I don't act like it's a big deal around them, maybe they won't feel so bad about it.* Some have even been so bold as to accuse the doctors of being wrong or to suggest that the diagnosis is incorrect.

Regardless of your intentions, please refrain. Minimizing a condition can be especially frustrating to someone who is dealing with a mental illness such as depression. It is not helpful to say things like "Just get over it!" or "What do you have to be depressed about?" or even "Count your blessings." Don't you think if they could "just get over it," they would? Depression is so much more than just being in a funk. Depression can be an extremely debilitating disease that sometimes makes getting out of bed a major accomplishment. It can also lead to many other illnesses and conditions, and it usually can't be cured with just a pill.

Making Jokes about Their Condition

Even if you have the best intentions and try to use humor as a pick-me-up, you might want to think twice about making comments that are meant to be funny. There's a good chance it's just too soon for jokes.

After returning to work following cancer treatment, for example, Doug was actually told, "You don't look sick; you just wanted a vacation." Even though he knew the person was joking, he found it a very insensitive thing to say. Likewise, Beth, who'd just had a double mastectomy, said that insensitive comments like "Now you'll have great boobs when you're older" really bothered her, despite knowing it was a bleak attempt at cheering her up.

While laughter is *usually* the best medicine, try to be aware that the patient might not be ready for personal jokes yet.

NOTES

_____

_____

_____

_____

_____

_____

_____

_____

_____

_____

_____

_____

_____

_____

_____

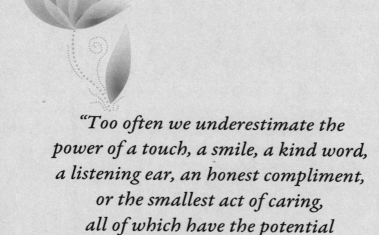

"Too often we underestimate the power of a touch, a smile, a kind word, a listening ear, an honest compliment, or the smallest act of caring, all of which have the potential to turn a life around."

—LEO BUSCAGLIA

CHAPTER 4

Helping in Times of Divorce and Unemployment

Divorce (or separation) and unemployment are two other potentially devastating situations that people face every day. I have several suggestions that I think you'll find useful for helping friends in either of these situations.

Divorce

Helping a friend who is going through a divorce can be very challenging for many reasons. While people don't choose to get sick or die, at least one of the partners involved does choose to get a divorce or separation. And despite how accepting modern society seems to be, there still can be a stigma attached to someone who is divorced. Divorced people may be seen as cheaters, gold diggers, liars, losers, victims, etc.

Complicated family issues can arise too. Family support might not be there as expected, and that can be very hurtful. In addition, friends and family often feel they have to choose a side, even if they're close with both spouses. This can be uncomfortable for those who want to remain friends with both people and don't want to be caught in the crossfire.

Divorce can be uncomfortable for the divorcing couple because they may be dealing with feelings of loss, anger, failure, and guilt. The feelings experienced during the process of a divorce can vary from day to day. One day, someone experiences loss and sorrow, and the next day, they may feel free and happy that the burden of a broken marriage has been lifted off their shoulders. A good friend is someone who will be there for them at their lowest lows and their highest highs, keeping an even temperament each time.

While some people see divorce as the best thing that has ever happened to them, others see it as a very painful event. Some people said having their ex-spouse actually die would be much easier to deal with because they would be gone. With divorce, their ex is alive and there's a chance of running into them and having to relive the pain each time. And when children are involved, these interactions with an ex-spouse can last a lifetime.

So, much care is needed to help those who find divorce painful through this tough time. Here are some things that could really help someone you care about when they are going through a divorce or separation:

- **Be there for them.** Although Keith's divorce was amicable, adjusting to it was still tough for him. He found having friends who were always willing to listen to him was very helpful. He also appreciated when his friends kept him busy with fun things to keep his mind off the divorce.

- **Spend the night or invite them to spend the night with you.** When Paula was going through her divorce, the hardest time for her was at night. "For me," she said, "it was difficult to be alone. It sounds strange, but nighttime or darkness was the absolute worst."

  The thought of being alone at night can be frightening or nerve wracking for many, especially for women who have never lived on their own before. Some may have moved from their parents' house or an apartment with friends directly into the home they shared with their spouse, and so they find themselves constantly on edge. For others, the long, dark nights give them too much time to think. Regardless of the reason, spending the night with a friend can provide them with a welcome break from their loneliness.

- **Invite them to hang out.** Running errands together might sound mundane to you, but to a friend who is lonely, it can be a welcome invitation to get out of the house, spend time with a friend, and shift their focus for a while.

- **Listen without judgment.** Many facing divorce constantly watch what they say and how they act in anticipation of how others will judge them. But almost every single person who responded to this survey said they needed someone to listen to them vent without the fear of being judged.

  Misty remembers that when she was going through her divorce, it was very comforting when her brother said to her, "'I don't care what happened or who did what to whom; I just want you to know that my heart is breaking for you.' When he said those words, I knew he wasn't passing judgment or trying to fix things. Instead, he acknowledged my traumatic experience and showed genuine, unbiased empathy." So remember, it's neither your job nor your business to determine who is right or wrong in this kind of instance. Your role is to be a friend by opening your ears and your heart. Listen.

- **Help them move or settle in to a new place.** During a divorce, one or both people in the marriage will be moving out of their home and setting up their life somewhere else. Offering to help them move can be beneficial in many ways. Extra bodies are always welcome for moving heavy furniture, but packing up old memories is often agonizing, so a friend's willingness to box things can alleviate some of the pain. And help in setting up their new household may be a great boost to someone who feels overwhelmed at this new chapter in life.

Unemployment

Your reactions to a friend or family member's unemployment issues can be complicated, depending on how they lost their job. For example, you may react differently to a friend who was laid off due to downsizing than to a friend who was fired for inappropriate conduct. You may be more willing to help the friend who just caught a "bad break" than a friend who you feel might have "gotten what he deserved." One situation might make you eager to reach out to help, while another situation might make you feel like running the other way.

Either way, losing a job can be devastating. Because so many people define who they are by what they do for a living, losing a job, regardless of the reason, can strike a blow to their identity as well as their ego. For some, it may just be about the loss of income—the partial or complete loss of income for them and their family. For others, it can be a blow to who they think they are, who they're trying to become, or who they're trying to convince others they are. Therefore, in addition to worries about no money coming in, there may be feelings of extreme fear, anger, sadness, and even shame.

If you do decide to reach out and help someone in this situation, I have some suggestions that I think you'll find helpful. The first and best thing you can do is to see if they want to talk about it. Then, be honest in asking what you might be able to do to help. If the person is open to having a conversation, you might be able to help them write a new resumé, or you might be able to provide a reference for them to use in their job search.

Not having a job probably means making different financial decisions—which means your friend might not be able to do the things they were used to doing. Just because they are cutting back does not mean you have to cut them out of your life. So continue to invite them out and let *them* make the decision whether to accept the invitation. While you might think it would be nice to offer to pick up the tab for dinner, be sure that is OK before you go out. Be clear in your invitation by asking if they would allow you to treat them to dinner. You might also want to offer a less expensive option, such as going to lunch instead of dinner.

Jody, who lost her job, said she felt very offended when friends would ask her to go to a movie and then pick up the tab. She said it made her feel as if she couldn't afford it, yet she found it just as insulting when friends wouldn't ask her out because they thought she couldn't afford to pay. So while you may have the best of intentions when offering to treat someone to a movie or dinner, you could easily offend them in the process. It may be best to set the ground rules before you go.

You can bypass these complications if you cook dinner for your friend or host a night of family fun. You can even offer to babysit so your friend can apply for jobs or go for interviews. You may also want to treat someone looking for new employment with a trip to the salon for a haircut and color or a manicure, as these might be some of the first luxuries cut from a budget.

Again, in this kind of situation, offering your friend or family member an honest, loving, caring conversation about how you can best support them might be the greatest thing you can do for them.

NOTES

_____

_____

_____

_____

_____

_____

_____

_____

_____

_____

_____

_____

_____

"Our prayers for others flow more easily than those for ourselves. This shows we are made to live by charity."

—C.S. LEWIS

"Showing up is what counts."

—GABRIELLE ZEVIN,
THE STORIED LIFE OF A. J.

CHAPTER 5

The Two Best Ways to Help Others Heal

I am extremely grateful for having so many people respond to my survey and for their willingness to share the most intimate details of their lives with me. Many have uncovered some old wounds in an effort to help others reach out in meaningful ways. This is a gift for which I will be eternally grateful. They have given me so many great suggestions to share in these pages—I hope you have been enlightened too.

Having studied every survey submitted to me, I have discovered two prominent actions others have used to help the respondents in their healing process—both of which have already been talked about: prayer and being there. Both bear repeating.

1. The Power of Prayer

The first is PRAYER. Roughly 98 percent of those surveyed said the prayers of others were helpful and meaningful to them. Here are some thoughts respondents offered regarding the power of prayer:

"The power of prayer is palpable,
and it's a method of support that sustains me
in any time of loss."

—ED

"I feel the prayers and depend on them."

—KAYE

"If you ever need to believe that there
is a higher power, a God, or a heaven,
it is when you have lost someone."

—JODY

"Prayers are such a private matter,
and to think that someone includes you
in their prayers is very special."

—MARIANN

"That someone would care enough to pray is
overwhelming."

—ANNE

"The fact that people are lifting me up in their prayers, thoughts, or whatever words we want to use is a positive thing, and all of that positive energy has to be good."

—MISTY

"I cherished every prayer as a gift."

—DOUG

"Knowing there are people outside of your family praying and giving you support is the best medicine in the world."

—BARB

2. Being There

The second common recommendation is something that is really sweet and simple and requires nothing more than one's presence: Just show up and be there for someone. Of all the suggestions in this book, this seems to be by far the MOST IMPORTANT thing someone can do to help someone they love who is going through life's toughest challenges. Yet though it seems simple enough, being there is something that can be very challenging for some.

Here are thoughts that some of those surveyed shared with me on being there:

"I believe that just letting someone know that they are loved and not alone and that you will be there for them is important."

—BARB

"Just be there with them. Even if they don't want to talk, let them know that things will get better."

—DIANE

"The single most important thing is to be there— be it phone calls, cards, e-mail, thoughts, prayers, flowers, cards, or gifts. Just being present in some way."

—BETH

"Get to that person, cry with them . . . be there. Do what you can to get there."

—DALE

"Listen. Be patient. Realize you can't fix it for them."

—MICHELLE

"Just be there, through it all . . . even if you don't know what to say! Just be there."

—BRADY

The Two Best Ways to Help Others Heal

"Be present. That's all that's needed."
—Wendy

"You have to be there for them—selflessly and unconditionally. And when you're there— BE THERE! Don't just show up to 'make an appearance.' Give them your whole heart, attention, and love."
—Lisa

As for my advice?

"Despite your fears, no matter your comfort zone, fight the urge to run the other way. Now is the time to step up and be a TRUE FRIEND."
—Sherrie

"May we reach out to one another in love, in faith, and in kindness."

LAILAH GIFTY AKITA,
THINK GREAT: BE GREAT!

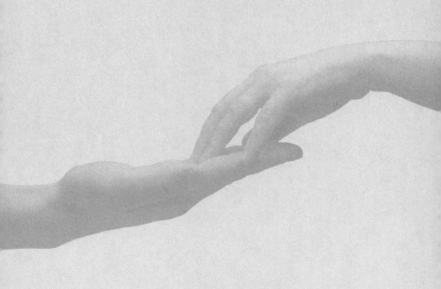

Conclusion

The entire reason for writing this book was to eradicate the excuse "I don't know what to say or do." That excuse does not get you off the hook. That excuse ruins relationships.

The suggestions you have just read have helped the people who have been kind enough to share the knowledge they've gained from their own painful experiences. So now that you've read through all the suggestions, go back and pick one or two that either feel natural or comfortable to you or that you know will mean something to your loved one who is suffering. Some of the suggestions might even trigger another great idea you can implement.

I want to thank you for reading this book! My biggest hope is to deepen human connections that lead to healing hearts and lives, so I hope you will use the suggestions in this book to help strengthen your bond with the person in need, and I hope that having read this book, you will never have to lose relationships simply because you did not know what to do in time of need.

I also hope you will continue to refer back to these pages as needed. And then—SHARE! Please share these ideas with others and share this book with them too. This guide is just as important to children leaving home as a good cookbook. It can help them develop deeper and more meaningful relationships with their friends and loved ones!

I know many of you who are reading this could be thinking back to a time when you suffered a loss, and you may even have a suggestion or two to add to this book. I would love to hear from you. I firmly believe that the more wonderful ideas we can share with each other, the better we will be able to serve one another. My goal is to get the conversation started and to provide a forum through which people can share ideas, such as what helped them most when they were going through a dark moment and/or what really helped them help someone else who was suffering. The point is to be able to provide a place where people can find something that will help them do something to help someone! Pretty basic and pretty simple—but VERY necessary.

If you have an idea you would like to share that is not included in this book, please feel free to contact me at sherriedunlevy@gmail.com. I would love to share your idea with others.

NOTES

NOTES

_____

_____

_____

_____

_____

_____

_____

_____

_____

_____

_____

_____

_____

_____

_____

_____

_____

_____

NOTES

_____

_____

_____

_____

_____

_____

_____

_____

_____

_____

_____

_____

_____

_____

_____

_____

_____

_____

_____

NOTES

_____

_____

_____

_____

_____

_____

_____

_____

_____

_____

_____

_____

_____

_____

_____

_____

_____

_____

About the Author

Sherrie Dunlevy is a wife and mother to two sons, one in heaven and one in college. She is also an entrepreneur and radio talk show host.

Sherrie works to make the world a better place by connecting people with ideas and concepts that are positive, loving, forward thinking, and based on human connection. She is passionate about living a life of meaning, love, dream building, and strong relationships.

Sherrie resides in Wheeling, West Virginia, with her husband and dog.